SWANSEA
THEN & NOW
IN COLOUR

GEOFF BROOKES

The
History
Press

This book is dedicated to our eight grandchildren,
Alex, Mr Will, Bethan, Sam, Isabelle, Emily, Jessica and Matilda.
Sorry kids, you can choose your friends
but you can't choose your family.
This is where your family comes from.
It might explain a lot.

First published in hardback 2012, this paperback edition 2015

The History Press
The Mill, Brimscombe Port
Stroud, Gloucestershire, GL5 2QG
www.thehistorypress.co.uk

© Geoff Brookes, 2012, 2015

The right of Geoff Brookes to be identified as the Author
of this work has been asserted in accordance with the
Copyright, Designs and Patents Act 1988.

British Library Cataloguing in Publication Data.
A catalogue record for this book is available from the British Library.

ISBN 978 0 7509 6503 3

Typesetting and origination by The History Press
Printed in China.

CONTENTS

ACKNOWLEDGEMENTS

The people of Swansea have made this book possible. They built this place after all, and many offered support whilst I was writing it.

My mother-in-law, Elaine Hopkin, has been an inspiration; she is full of lots of useful information, especially about the east side. My old friend Eileen Bristow has been very supportive, and knows many unusual things about Brynhyfryd and Landore. My insight into the peculiar goings-on in Cockett comes from Phil Mattey and his sister Mary, who have lived there, in the same house, for the whole of their eighty-eight years. Phil took me on a tour around the site of Cockett Pond and snuffled around in the bushes until he found one of the bricks made from Cockett clay by the now gone Tunnel Brickworks – thank you, Phil.

Of course, I could not have made this book without the interest and patience of the staff in the West Glamorgan Archive Service in the Swansea Civic Centre. They nod, they smile and they shake their heads very gently before easing a file out from their shelves to keep me happy. They know what they are doing, unlike me.

The people of Swansea have been very understanding. They have been interested and supportive, especially when I was out taking pictures and they realised I wasn't from the council, and that I wasn't planning to park diggers in their gardens. I have had many interesting conversations. I would like to thank the children of Gowerton for standing still long enough to allow me to take a photograph. Bethan, Chloe and Dan, along with their chums Kieran and Ryan, helped me to think about how the lives of children have changed beyond all recognition. The people I work with at Education Effectiveness have tolerated my obsessive conversations with their exemplary patience; I thank them for this.

Often it seems wet in the original photos, so I would like to thank very sincerely the weather gods who have looked so kindly on my work. As you can see, in my photographs the weather was generally good. Such an absence of rain in Swansea is quite remarkable. It rains here more than in any other UK city apparently. And don't we know it!

INTRODUCTION

This book reflects the remarkable work of the Borough Engineer's Department. What a fantastic job they did, carefully cataloguing their work as they maintained the inadequate structure of the town around them. Their photographs are an unrivalled resource about the past. Every one is fascinating. A record of work ordered, planned, and completed. The details of everyday life: improvements, repairs, demolition. For them, this was their work, their day. What they did between cups of tea. For us it is a wonderful resource and without them this book would be so much poorer.

Their pictures represent a record of social history. They were often taken for an entirely different purpose, which gives them an honesty and a purity not found in staged or planned photos. They are a window into the past.

These pictures tell a story about how the place where we live has changed, and how we have adapted our surroundings and ourselves to new circumstances and needs. This is a record of the out-of-town places, the unconsidered places. Our history, it seems to me, lies in the stones and in the walls that we pass every day.

There have been times when it has been difficult to take the contemporary pictures. It is not that you can't find the location. That is usually very easy. The problem is the ubiquitous influence of the car. They either head madly towards the innocent photographer, driven by his art to stand in the middle of the road, or they litter the roadside obscuring everything. Such are the times we live in.

So let me take you on a journey through our lovely ugly town. This is Dylan Thomas's famous phrase but he could never have anticipated how his Swansea would be changed – always with the best of intentions but not always for the better. So we will start in the west, down in Mumbles, and then follow a peculiar route back through Swansea to finish at the station.

Any place needs to be in touch with its own past. Even when much of the past has been destroyed, we still have a need to find out where we came from and, perhaps, where we are going.

VILLAGE LANE

WE START OUR journey through Swansea in Village Lane in Mumbles. It runs down very steeply from Higher Lane to the seafront on Mumbles Road. It is a beautiful place, with great character and atmosphere. It reminds one that Mumbles is a holiday resort. This pair of photographs represents the transition of Mumbles from a simple fishing village, known for oyster dredging, to a smart and desirable suburb. Village Lane is one of a warren of streets and lanes beneath the Mumbles Hill Local Nature Reserve.

The early photograph from the Swansea Archive appears to be from the nineteenth century but is in fact from 1929. Even so, it still represents a lost world.

Mumbles was for centuries a separate village to which access was not easy. For generations, the only way to access it was along the beach. Benjamin Heath Malkin's book *The Scenery, Antiquities and Biography of South Wales* from 1804 says, 'The village is singularly situated under the shadow of a high limestone rock and it still gathers itself around the bulk of Mumbles Head.'

Of course, to the delight of all Swansea schoolboys, the name Mumbles is thought to derive from the French word *mamelles*, meaning breasts, and refers to the two rocks off the head (accessible at low tide for those who are careful). The name of the parish has always been Oystermouth, but now those two names are interchangeable. Certainly either is easier to pronounce for visitors than the Welsh, Ystumllwynarth.

Mumbles has always lived with the sea. It is a fishing village, noted for its oysters, and is the home to the famous and courageous Mumbles lifeboat crew. Today it is a place for leisure, for cafés, restaurants, walks and surfing on the other side of the headland.

Village Lane has been slightly remodelled, as you can see if you look at the roofs in the new photograph, but it is largely untouched and nothing could ever take away the fantastic views you get across Swansea Bay from here, or from along the front below.

NEWTON ROAD

WE HAVE MOVED now to the central crossroads in Mumbles, where Mumbles Road meets Newton Road. This junction on the front was known as the Dunns. This photograph was taken prior to redevelopment in 1970; it is remarkable to see the changes that have taken place.

In 1970 the road surface seems uneven, untended. The road is narrow and dark. The houses on the left have clearly come to the end of their time. The scene is unwelcoming, almost threatening; it is a crossroads in decay.

When we look at it now there is enough detail in the background to show that this is the same place, but the differences are significant. Today everything is smarter and cleaner, suggesting comfort and relaxation. The changes have opened up the view. And of course, the sunshine always helps Mumbles to look its best.

Mumbles – the village apart. A place where some Swansea people want to live and where others would rather not. It is a steep, compact holiday destination, tumbling down to the sea at the end of a busy road from Swansea. It is a lovely place, although, to be truthful, the weather that sweeps

in off the bay isn't terribly helpful at times and the traffic has the capacity to be nightmarish on a daily basis.

It certainly has all the ingredients for a fine Welsh resort. A lighthouse was erected in 1793 on the outer of the two islands and a pier was built in 1898. There is an underlying sense of cheerfulness, of people enjoying their life along the shore, in their boats – fishing when the tide comes in – and relaxing in the bars and restaurants after. It is the location of a series of pubs known as the Mumbles Mile, a scenic stagger through some of the old haunts of Dylan Thomas.

There is history too. It was probably the site of a Roman villa, as the pieces of a mosaic pavement which remain in All Saints' Church suggest. And if you turn up the road at this junction you will come to Oystermouth Castle. Malkin says that 'it is a majestic ruin ... commanding a delightful prospect of the country'. He was right then, and he still is today. And these days you don't need to be a lord to enjoy the pleasures of Mumbles.

MAYALS ROAD

TRAVEL TOWARDS SWANSEA and you reach the junction between Mayals Road and Mumbles Road. It is 1965; we know it is the sixties because we can see a bubble car sweeping majestically round the corner on its way to Swansea. It is not a vehicle that other decades ever embraced.

A policeman on duty directs the traffic, his white gauntlets designed to make his gestures more visible. We have to manage on our own these days, as you can see. Road markings may be

more efficient and cheaper, and I certainly wouldn't want to stand like that in the middle of the road, but traffic lights and bollards have less personality and interest, in my view.

Turn inland from where the policeman stands and you will find that Mayals Road has an air of comfort about it. It runs alongside the beautiful Clyne Gardens and then onwards to Bishopston and South Gower. From this road the prosperous descend to the congestion of Mumbles Road on their daily commute. As you can see, things were not that different in 1965.

The popular pub, the Woodman, remains untouched and the wall on the corner is much the same; the trees are more mature, that is all.

Behind the crossroads you will find Clyne Gardens, famous for its rhododendrons. The gardens have a long history. The oak woodland is a reminder of Clyne Forest, popular with the Normans. The castle was originally built in 1791 and was bought by William Vivian in 1860; he developed the gardens. The gardens boast the tallest magnolia in the country and is blessed with a bog garden, elephant rhubarb and American skunk cabbage, which is naturally a big draw. There is plenty to see and the chapel is lovely too.

On the other side of the road by the sea you can find the Junction, once the generating station for the Mumbles Railway, fronting the space where the rails once were. Many would love to see the railway restored.

SINGLETON PARK

WE HAVE MADE a slight detour to Singleton Park to visit the crazy golf course, and to pay brief homage to the Mumbles Railway.

One of the few things that unite the people of Swansea is the frequently expressed opinion that the Mumbles Railway should never have been closed. Hindsight remains a wonderful thing. At the time it was a response to the seductive freedom offered by the motor car. Why wait for a tram when you could drive home in your own time? Take it away, widen the road. Today that seems touchingly naïve, as those of us who have spent too long in traffic on Mumbles Road

will confirm. Undeniably it would be an important tourist attraction if it had survived, but others didn't see the world in the same way.

And of course the more cynical amongst you might say that if it was so wonderful then why didn't people use it more frequently? The company running it was making a loss. Romantic visions are fine, but they do not always make business sense.

The first meeting of the shareholders of the Mumbles Railway took place at the Bush Inn in High Street. The railway began in 1804 and was designed to service the quarries and coal mines in Clyne. By 1807 passengers were being carried. It was the inspiration for a number of odd ideas – such as the scheme to harness the power of wind by equipping the trains with sails. Initially it was drawn by horses, then by steam, and finally it was electrified in 1927. It was very popular immediately after the Second World War; in 1946 it carried over 4 million passengers. The last train home on a Saturday night would have hundreds clinging to the outside. Sadly, however, its popularity faded and the end was inevitable. The last journey was in January 1960.

It is almost impossible to write a book about Swansea without mentioning the Mumbles Railway. It now has almost mythical status, an enduring folk memory. There is a replica in the National Waterfront Museum. But the only photograph I will offer you is of a (disappeared) model on a crazy golf course in Singleton Park in 1965. Perhaps that tells you everything you need to know.

SKETTY HALL

IF YOU GO now to the top of Sketty Lane, beyond Singleton
Hospital, you will find Sketty Hall. It is a place with a long and
distinguished history. The photograph was taken in 1969, when
it was all rather faded and worn. Now, as you can see, it has been
sensitively and beautifully restored.

The hall was originally built in the 1720s by Raleigh Dawkin
and at one time it was owned by Charles Baring, of the famous
merchant banking family in London. It was sold to Lewis Weston
Dillwyn, owner of the Cambrian Pottery in Swansea. His family
were delighted – they said that Sketty Hall was 'very quiet and
retired.' Later it passed into the hands of Richard Vivian. You
will notice that the famous names of Swansea's history run
through the whole of Sketty's past – in the ownership of the
hall and in the names of the roads. During the Second World
War, the hall was a Civil Defence Headquarters, which is how
it is described by the Borough Engineers when they took their
picture. It also served time as a facility for the British Iron and
Steel Research Association.

The building was restored in 1994–95 and is currently
operated by Gower College; it is some sort of solutions and

innovations centre, as well as a place for weddings and retirement dinners, like my own. As you can see when you compare the two pictures, the transformation is impressive.

Once restored it became a popular venue. The gardens at the back are especially attractive and loved by wedding photographers. In summer the whole of the house opens up and it seems to draw inside all the pleasures of the sun.

Within there are elegant rooms, with fine fireplaces and a wonderful staircase. You get a clear sense of what it would have been like to live in a grand house overlooking the sea.

We will move on now, past Bishop Gore School, to Sketty Cross.

SKETTY CROSS

SKETTY GREW UP around this busy crossroads. Sketty Cross was the intersection of two important routes, one heading to Mumbles and the other leading to Gower. At the start of the twentieth century the roads here were not laid, with uneven slabs bridging the open gutters. It was undoubtedly a separate village but it was very soon drawn into the town. Westward expansion and the building of housing estates took away any sense of rural isolation. The roads were widened and redeveloped to accommodate the growing population. It was always a prosperous place. As Malkin's guidebook said in 1804, 'it is on an eminence, commanding the whole of Swansea Bay'. Where else would the residents ever want to be? Now it has pockets of high-density housing.

At one point there was a pub on each corner of the Cross. This kept patrons safe from the dangers of crossing unmade roads in the dark by providing them with their very own place. However, the Cross Inn and the New Inn have disappeared. But the roads still carry the mark of history. They enshrine famous names from Swansea's past – Dillwyn Road, Vivian Road.

There is a modest collection of shops on the Cross now: takeaway restaurants, hairdressers, grocers, locksmiths. But there is also a very important part of the Swansea heritage – Nash Sports. An unassuming sports shop, but one which reminds many of us of that legendary occasion when Malcolm Nash – proprietor – ran up to the crease to bowl for Glamorgan against Nottinghamshire's captain, Gary Sobers, in 1968.

Sketty Cross seems to have maintained its square and angular character. The old façade had a little more interest but the new one has cleaner, neater edges. The Odeon cinema, which had originally opened under the name of the Maxime in 1938, was once on the left-hand side where Lloyds bank is now. This shows you just how much more sophisticated they are in the west. In Morriston, one of our cinemas has become a tyre and exhaust centre.

VIVIAN ROAD

THIS IS CLOSE to Sketty Cross, 100 yards or so along Vivian Road. Perhaps the most important thing about this picture is the fact that things haven't changed much at all. The original image was taken in the 1930s, eighty years ago, but all is still recognisable.

Vivian Road has a different role now, taking traffic down not only from Townhill but also from the west, down towards Mumbles and Singleton Hospital. It is a main route now. Just up the hill you will find the Tycoch campus of Gower College ,which brings so many people to the area. Not just from Swansea – students attend from across the world.

It is interesting to see how those lovely houses have remained untouched. The road too is the same shape and size, although now it has a different name. At the time it was Townhill Road, but after the junction with Glanmor Road was redesigned it became Vivian Road.

It might be wide from here up the hill, but back towards the Cross it is narrow and there is a permanent queue at the traffic lights, which must be irritating for the residents.

The photographs provide an interesting contrast. In the older picture there is a pedestrian but no cars. The new picture is the polar opposite – cars aplenty but no people.

We can just see a National Garage at the extreme right of the frame. Today it is a renowned angling shop. On the opposite side, the house on the corner with Kimberley Road was then a fish 'n' chip shop. Now it is a hairdresser's.

Sketty has always been one of the favoured suburbs, protected from the toxic outpourings of the Swansea Valley. It was to Sketty that the factory owners came to build their homes.. Down by the sea there was Singleton Abbey, built by John Henry Vivian, which later became the University College of Swansea. There were other wealthy families in Sketty and they brought with them their domestic servants. Soon small businesses gathered around them to service their needs. That sense of prosperity is still present.

EDGEWARE ROAD

WE HAVE MADE a slight detour along Glanmor Road to look at an advertisement. What we are looking at here is Edgeware Road, which joins Glanmor Road, opposite where the girls' school used to be. There is no date on the early photograph but it would seem to be in the 1930s. The skyline is uncluttered, with an organised uniformity to the chimneys. There is just a bicycle propped up on the kerb of a deserted street. There is a rather ghostly feel too, in the emptiness before you.

This photograph was taken because the council were getting excited by the advertisement on the wall. They felt it was too bold, a little garish perhaps. The houses are clean and neat but Greta Colday seems to be looming down on the world in a way that was regarded as rather too intrusive.

When you first glance at the modern photograph nothing much seems to have changed although, of course, the advertising hoarding has gone. But there are other more subtle changes in the contemporary picture. The houses have more individuality and a sense of ownership. There are no bikes on show now, just cars on both sides of the road. Today the houses wear satellite dishes, aerials, and of course stench pipes, indicating that finally the toilets have moved inside. The wall on the corner is substantially the same but now looks out on to a road that has street lamps, traffic management and speed cameras. Welcome to our world – and whilst we have been building it, Edgeware Road has continued to provide happy homes for the people who live there.

And what about Greta Colday? She was a made-up name as far as I know. A play on words, tapping into the enthusiasm for the cinema and glamorous film stars. Think about it: Greet a Cold Day with a cup of Oxo! Such an invitation.

In those days you had to make your own entertainment.

TYCOCH SQUARE

WE HAVE NOW retraced our steps slightly, back to Vivian Road, past Gower College and on to Tycoch Square.

Tycoch lies to the north of Sketty woodlands and is known locally for the location of one of the campuses of the new Gower College (the other campus is in Gorseinon). The long steep hill is home to a number of housing developments, some of which have quite spectacular views.

The older photograph is undated (it almost certainly dates from around 1938) but it rewards careful study. The cinema advertised on the wall of the house on the corner of Llywn Afrosa road, was down at Sketty Cross, where we saw its shadow in the buildings. It originally opened in 1938 as the Maxime and later became the Odeon.

There is a bicycle with a basket parked against the kerb. Close by there is a schoolboy with a cap, short trousers and long socks, looking at the camera as people did in those days. There is a blurred figure going into the shop called Tycoch Library. Above the bank you can see children looking out of the window. No such domestic arrangement would be permitted these days. Above Tycoch Library is a unisex hairdresser.

Of course there has been an obvious change in the nature of the shops, which is telling of our modern priorities. The cinema advertisement has been replaced by one for a garage and for a laundrette, which will provide an ironing service for busy people. There is a tanning shop and next door is still the site of a hairdresser's, but today it has moved downstairs.

A wall has been removed to open up the front for the cleaners and its parking needs. The skyline is less uniform too but you can still see an original chimney, now augmented by our essential electronic devices.

But the most significant item in either picture is the police box. What a reassuring and beautiful piece of architecture it was, and what an obvious symbol of a vanished time.

GOWER ROAD

YOU HAVE TRAVELLED now to Gower Road in Killay – or Cila. The name relates to an ancient battle and means a place of retreat. It was probably the same battle referred to at Llewitha Bridge. And quite an appropriate name when you consider the number of people who retire here. It is high above sea level and has its own nature reserve alongside the River Clyne. At one time it was a mining village, with a large number of collieries running down towards Dunvant. But slowly Swansea has stretched out to embrace Killay. Now it indicates to drivers that they have returned after their Sunday afternoon drive. You drive back from Gower, you cross the cattle grid by the rugby club and you are back in the city. You come up the hill past St Hilary's Church (where there are twenty-four war graves of those who served on Fairwood Common during the war) to the roundabout at the Siloam Baptist Chapel, and you will see the Commercial public house on the right.

It is a well-known and popular landmark and in the photographs it appears untouched by time. The earlier photo is undated but you can see that the outline of the building hasn't changed very much. Other things have. There is certainly more elegance to the older street lamp. There is a pavement now, whereas before the road was narrower, and half the size of what it is today. As you can see, to take the picture I stood in the central reservation, which was once the other pavement, and which for me was very welcome as a safe vantage point. It is a busy place and parking can be a challenge. The garden wall in front of where the shop once was is more substantial now. It might be blander but it is neater, and it fronts one smart house rather than two cottages. The shop has gone altogether, along with the signs positioned to catch the eye of those heading into Swansea.

The advertisements caused some complaints, especially the ones for dog cakes and puppy biscuits. Of course, times were sometimes hard in the past, but I must assume that the adverts indicate their intended consumers rather than their ingredients.

GOWERTON

WE HAVE TRAVELLED down through Dunvant and arrived at the gateway to the glories of
Gower. This is the square in Gowerton, which is called Market Square in the original postcard.

You are standing on Mount Street in these photographs, looking down towards Gorseinon. The
buildings are the same, though their use has changed. As have people's attitudes towards cameras.
All of these children are appearing in order to watch the camera, in their smocks and caps. Their
friends are hurrying along Mill Street to find out what is happening. Today their descendants have
telephones with cameras and their lives are full of casually taken images. But the roads are not for
them. My friends here, Bethan and Chloe on the right, and Kieran, Dan and Ryan on the left, must
always watch out for the traffic. No casual playing for them in the square. Cars are the enemy
of children.

Gowerton is an interesting example of an old mining community, proud of its industrial heritage. A place of coal mines, steelworks and tinplate works. Today there is little hint of these industrial roots, although the pit is remembered, for the name Elba crops up everywhere.

Today the square is a busy junction. Traffic from Gorseinon chooses either to turn left to Swansea or right to Gower, whilst the people park as best they can in order to take the cat to the vet or to have their hair cut.

The shop directly in front of us was originally the grocer's Lloyd Morgan. Today it is a veterinary practice. The living accommodation above housed Belgian refugee families during the First World War. Later it became part of the Co-op Stores.

On the left there is the Welcome to Gower Inn, which dates from 1857. It was the accepted meeting place of local farmers and landowners.

This was a particularly boggy area, but the sinking of a colliery shaft dried the area out and enabled cottages to be built. Better subsidence than flooding, apparently.

The miners' cottages are still there but Gowerton was always regarded as a place for managers. The people were thus known as the Starch. The workers who came from Penclawdd were known generally as the Donks – an insult which has survived the passage of time. Of course, when the mists drift in from the estuary, you can sometimes find that your sense of humour is hard to locate.

COCKETT POND

I THINK THIS is a fascinating picture and a forgotten piece of our heritage. We have travelled back through Waunarlwydd along the B4295 to Cockett. The photograph here is of Cockett Pond, behind St Peter's Terrace, and it shows the fire brigade attempting to drain it in September 1958. A local youth had tragically drowned. He was not the first. The earliest recorded accident dates from November 1876 when William Davies, an eight year old, fell from a plank on which he was playing. Later a group of wild ducks settled on the pond and a man came from Fforestfach to shoot them. He fell in and drowned. Another four deaths were recorded before 1939.

The pond was formed as a clay pit, when clay was used to supply the local Tunnel Brickworks in Cwmdu. There are so many springs in the area that any hole quickly fills with water, as this one did. Cockett Pond was remarkably deep (apparently 96ft at one point), steep sided and with unstable banks.

The local Swansea and District Coarse Fishing Club looked after the water, stocking it with carp smuggled in on bicycles from other local ponds. But for others it had a more fatal fascination.

The water at the top was usually relatively warm, whilst the spring water was freezing cold beneath. This could cause cramps and in some cases drowning. It was so easy for reckless boys to dive in – and so difficult for them to scramble out.

There were other dangers too. The local boys would hold lighted paper on sticks and ignite the escaping bubbles that broke the surface. They would explode and sounded like machine guns. This was methane from the coal seams. You hope that methane has now dispersed.

Of course, you can't see anything of the pond. The outline of the houses along Ael y Bryn Road is the only thing there is to match past and present, for the rest has disappeared. The pond has been filled in and houses have been built on top of it, in what some might regard as a rather reckless fashion. But it is remembered in the unkempt green area next to the railway line which has the name Cockett Pond on a sign. It must be so confusing for some, for it is hard to imagine anywhere that looks less like a pond than this place where people now tether their sad and neglected horses.

COCKETT

FROM THE SITE of the pond we have come to the top of Cockett Road, to the junction with Waunarlwydd Road, and have stopped to look across at Lon Towy, which in the earlier photograph was a building site, as you can see. This undated picture seems to have been taken in the 1930s.

When you look at the present-day picture, you are reminded that you can't change the landscape too much. The hill is still there. Now it is green and growing; then it was mud and lorries – solid and

full of business. There is a sign on the mound too, to the left. It advertises the Cockett Road Estate: 'Desirable Semi Detached Houses For Sale; £587.' You will be pleased to learn that mortgages can be arranged. The builder was Syd Davies of Sketty.

The origins of the name Cockett are unclear. Once this was a heavily wooded area so perhaps the name links to the Welsh for cuckoo, *Gog wig*. As a result it could mean the cuckoo's flying ground. But no one is really sure.

In the nineteenth century this was the most highly developed coal-producing area. There were significant pits at Weig Fawr and at Gorse, and their tunnels snake everywhere underneath Cockett. It is a place too of a multitude of natural springs, which gives homeownership here an unwelcome sense of adventure. A number of housing estates were developed as industry declined and now it is an area with a wide range of homes.

Cockett has always seen itself as a village separate from Swansea. Perhaps it also felt that the same laws didn't apply to them. In March 1876 the licensee of the Cockett Inn, John Williams, was fined £1 for serving beer out of hours. Poor Mr Gibbs had needed a drink after a 4-mile walk from Swansea in sleet and snow, so Williams served him. An act of undoubted charity, but of course in those days you were only allowed to be thirsty at certain times of the day.

GYPSY CROSS

THIS IS ONE of those places in Swansea that we all tend to overlook.
We have travelled along the narrow, twisting Waunarlwydd Road, past
Cefn Coed Hospital and down to cross the B4295 along which we came
from Gowerton. The early photograph was taken on a wet winter's day
in 1966 and, as you can see from the contemporary picture, things
haven't changed a great deal. The undergrowth might be a little
denser but that is all.

This is known as Gypsy Cross. Cockett has had a long and fruitful
relationship with Romany Gypsies and a field nearby was, until
recently, the home of Bobby Lee and his sister Anita, who were popular
local figures. Their home was the village of Cockett, amongst its
independently minded people. Cockett has always been a place apart.

In front you can see the road we have just come down, quite
unsuited to the modern world. We have tried to adapt it to our
needs but with little success. It speaks of another time. It was
a single-track road along which grannies used to take their
grandchildren to pick wild strawberries. Today it is a place where the
white van man can drive you off the road into a ditch as he thunders

round the corner, late for his next delivery, or where feral youths driving stolen motorcycles can crash into your car.

Yet this was once the main road. To the right there is Waunarlwydd – the Lords Meadow. A coal-mining village like so many others. Its prominence as a centre for the manufacture of zip fasteners and as the site of an Alcoa factory has long since gone. Now it is a long, spread-out village, separating Gowerton from Swansea.

The crossroads is used much more than it used to be by those hoping to avoid traffic delays. Ystrad Road, from where the photographs were taken, leads through the industrial estate to Fforesthall and you can, on a good day, miss the traffic in Fforestfach. A left turn at Gypsy Cross can sometimes bring you luck.

LLEWITHA BRIDGE

WE HAVE GONE through the industrial estate and turned left just before Fforesthall towards Gorseinon, and travelled about 400m.

Look at the early picture. This is the old bridge that crosses the River Llan on Carmarthen Road (B4620) on the way to Loughor. It was taken in 1930. When you look at such pictures it can be a shock to realise how isolated some places were at that time. On the hill to the right you can see Garngoch No.1 pit, which was part of the group of mines owned by Glasbrook. They employed over 900 men in their time. There was an explosion on 7 July 1880 when the pit was being worked with naked lights. Six men were killed, the youngest being Daniel Watkins who was fourteen. All the pits in the area were prone to the influx of gas.

Of course, over the years the area has become part of the urban spread of Swansea and is less rural. But the past is there in these pictures. Developments have actually restored the road's connection with its past. Now that it is straight, it more resembles the original Roman road that lies beneath the modern surface, which joined the settlements at Neath and Loughor.

In 970 the area was the site of a highly important battle, from which nearby Cadle takes its name – 'place of battle'. Prince Einon, after whom Gorseinon is named, was unhorsed and killed in a bog near Penllergaer. Lyn Cadwgan, leader of the western tribes, was killed whilst drinking from a well just off to the right of the bridge. It is a part of Swansea with a long, important and sadly overlooked history. Up at the top of the road near the old colliery is the site of the Battle of Garngoch in 1136, a significant battle in Welsh history when the Norman settlers were comprehensively defeated.

Of course the Llan doesn't seem much to us, as we thunder across, but any bridging point was important. Sadly any sense of a bridge has long disappeared in a functional roadway across the river. Most people won't even know that they are crossing a bridge. There are trees now and there is no need to dwell too long, which is a shame. The place has stories to tell.

PONTARDDULAIS ROAD

WE HAVE RETURNED from Llewitha, up Carmarthen Road to the junction with Pontarddulais Road. We have emerged where the Ford Anglia is launching itself across the road, though these days this junction is blocked. It was the old Roman road that becomes Middle Road on the other side of the junction.

In 1966 there was no need for traffic lights, though the position of the cars seems to suggest rather casual attitudes, both to priority at junctions and to parking; simpler times, obviously.

Cadle Primary School, which you can see on the left, has since been relocated just out of shot, next to the excellent Community Farm.

The large white building to the right was once a notable public house, the Ivorites Arms. It was named after the Philanthropic Order of True Ivorites, the only nineteenth-century friendly society that conducted its business in Welsh. Its objectives were to support the poor and the Welsh language. They had their own hand signals and handshakes, which all secret societies should embrace in my view. Their name had nothing at all to do with elephants. They took their name from Ifor Hael, who was the patron of the Welsh medieval poet Dafydd ap Gwilym.

A rather more noble use of an elegant building than a fashion outlet, but then perhaps I am just old.

An out-of-town shopping experience is available today to the right – it is something that characterises our times, something that has had a negative impact on the city centre and something that disenfranchises those who do not own cars. It is always busy because it solves problems we believe we have. It draws people to the roads of Fforestfach in their cars and thus changes the shape of the city.

The Ivorites were encouraged to show unity and fraternity and to assist each other in sickness and adversity. This is not the mission statement of any of the concerns in the retail park, as far as I understand them. Perhaps the world really is a poorer place.

MYNYDD NEWYDD ROAD

WE HAVE COME along Middle Road and arrived at Ravenhill. This is the junction with Pentregethin Road, one of the long and ancient roads of Swansea that cuts a route through to the north-west in Cadle.

You can use the bus garage to orientate yourself. It is still there, though clearly it is much larger than it used to be. You can use the square building on the left too. Today it is a bookmaker's. It is the area around these two landmarks that has changed so much.

The old photograph was taken in 1938 and pre-dates the development of the area. You could be in the middle of west Wales, rather than in Swansea.

A common feature in many of these older pictures is the way in which the countryside extended its long fingers into the modern city until quite recently. Then suddenly everything changed very quickly. What we see here is a very different place. It is what lies hidden beneath the concrete and the tarmac, which we have used to tame the environment.

This is an important junction today. It is rarely quiet. Now it needs to be controlled by traffic lights to give pedestrians a chance. It is the sort of junction that mothers are afraid to let their children cross alone. And yet how would they have felt in 1938?

There is an interesting contrast here too. On one hand, a quiet and untroubled scene with a bus garage, representing a motorised and a connected future. Yet the garage is surrounded by the sort of single-track roads a car would struggle to negotiate. Did they really take buses along these lanes?

Look at the track in front of you leading off across the common towards the traffic lights at Tirdeunaw. You can't imagine it ever becoming a proper road.

And yet there are signs. There is rubble in the middle of the picture and improvements to the road are taking place – unstoppable progress. And soon all this was lost.

GENDROS CRESCENT

WE HAVE TURNED right on to Pentregethin Road and then made our
way into Gendros. This is a fascinating photograph. You are standing
on Upper Gendros Crescent, looking towards Carmarthen Road. This is
the junction with Middle Road and on the other side you enter Gendros
Crescent. It is 1967 and the road is unmade, despite the cars which
are clearly using it. Not a great deal has changed in over forty years.

One instinctively looks to the massed rows of the Townhill Estate.
The estate was first developed as Homes for Heroes, intended to house
returning soldiers from the First World War in decent conditions. The
first dwellings were built on the other side of the hill, in Mayhill, and the
development on this side was subject to a number of delays. The initial
contract in 1919 was for 150 homes in blocks of six, designed to be as
picturesque as they were prominent. It was awarded to Rogers & Davies
of Cardiff, who submitted the cheapest tender at just under £762 per
house. However, they proved difficult to work with and eventually the
contract was taken over by a London company, Robert Young.

They insisted on a clause being added to the contract indicating that the council would provide insurance against damage through riots. These were volatile times and they obviously feared the contagion of the Russian Revolution taking an unwelcome grip in Wales. Either that or they had completely the wrong idea about the character of future Townhill residents.

That contract failed too and in the end Swansea Council built the houses itself and the first 150 were completed in 1922. Then, flushed with success, they went on to build more – as any visitor to Swansea will see. The houses themselves and the environment they are in have been upgraded and the community continues to thrive. But the shape of Townhill remains the same as it has always been.

DAVID STREET

WE HAVE MOVED down towards Cwmbwrla and just before the roundabout we have found David Street. It links Manselton to Pentregethin Road and is a short, undistinguished street, but for the older reader this picture represents our childhood. This is what the world looked like when we were young. It was a succession of small terraced houses, street after street, each a home, each part of a small community. Swansea had many such places.

The photograph was taken in 1965 and shows the odd-numbered houses on the left side of the road prior to demolition. You will find that the houses on the right-hand side have survived and remain neat and well cared for. But these houses have gone, as has, presumably, the lonely dog. The street has been remodelled and seems more open. But the shape of the street is still there. We have, of course, replaced one type of uniformity with another, but have removed the decay and the risks that such houses came to represent.

The open land that you can just see at the bottom on the right is still there, and so is that interesting façade on the right on Cae Bricks Street that once was white. At one time it was a garage, and then a glazier's; now it is a tea shop on the corner of one of Swansea's forgotten streets, behind Cwmbwrla roundabout.

At the top of the picture you can see the Bethel Welsh Baptist Chapel, but that has now gone.

In Swansea you can see how these houses were designed to keep workers uncomplaining and locked into their employment, especially when you move further towards the Lower Swansea Valley in Hafod, Landore and Pentrechwyth. If the factory owned them then you would be more inclined to be subservient, rather than risk eviction in an area where there was no alternative accommodation.

David Street was home to a mix of professions in the nineteenth century. Census details indicate coal merchants, tube workers, dock labourers, smelters, and railway engineers. A short street perhaps, but one with a place in the development of our city.

LION STREET

THIS IS LION STREET in Waun Wen, which lies between Carmarthen Road and Llangyfelach Street. It isn't very far from David Street. In August 1875 a shop, previously in the possession of Mr Skinner, was auctioned for an annual ground rent of £2 4s. The advertisement said it was a healthy locality and a growing district in the vicinity of extensive works, which would prove to be a good investment.

By the time the photo was taken in 1964 the houses had served their purpose and were ready to go. Lion Street has always had excellent views, and in comparing the backgrounds of both pictures, you can see the way Swansea has changed. In the earlier picture you can see the scars from industry and faintly the smoke from distant chimneys. Waun Wen means 'white meadow'; hardly appropriate at that time. In the centre of the picture you can see the enormous mass of Pentremawr tip.

Now, Lion Street is neater and the view is very different indeed. You can see the Liberty Stadium, the shared home of rugby and football. You may also notice how much greener it is.

Census data from the nineteenth century tells you about the people who lived there. Families were large and lived in small houses.

They were almost entirely English-speaking and came from many different places, like Chepstow, Carmarthen, and Ireland, all drawn by the work available in Swansea.

An interesting range of occupations could be found in Lion Street in 1891. One resident was a time keeper in the lead works, one an assistant in a metallurgical laboratory, while another was a blacksmith's striker. You will also find a girl of thirteen who was employed as a domestic servant.

The original residents were very proud of their new homes and they fed and sheltered the police when they staked out Jane Cole's brothel in 1877. When police forced entry in the early hours, they found a number of drunken sailors, and Jane Cole attacked a policeman with a shovel. As the Chief Constable later said in court – after Jane had been sentenced to one month's hard labour – it was wrong that such a place should exist in a respectable street between the school and the convent.

EVANS TERRACE

EVANS TERRACE LIES on the other side of the main road and is a real window into the past. We are on Wilks Row, looking along Evans Terrace in Mount Pleasant in 1957. The usual bicycle is propped against the kerb, unlocked. There is a sense of a living community, with doors opening straight on to the street, children playing, and people busy with their own lives. There are attractive street lamps and there is an openness about the view.

The road layout is the same today, but to be honest it is hard to imagine that anyone could ever think of changing it. The whole area seems precariously attached to the steep hillside. Short Street, a little further up the hill, ends abruptly at the foot of a rock face. There is always a feeling that this mass of tight little roads is going to fall down the hill. The views are fantastic but you need to have unshakable confidence in your handbrake, and as you approach a corner hope fervently that no one is coming towards you. Driving around up here isn't easy. Many of the roads are one-way and you must circulate carefully. Roads are blocked off for safety and slip steeply out of sight.

In the background you can see North Hill Road, which swoops down to Dyfatty. It was on North Hill that the hangman's gibbet stood 1,000 years ago.

When you look at the contemporary photograph you can see that some of the houses remain the same, especially further along the terrace. Houses on both sides of the road appear untouched by time. Closer to the camera there is perhaps a sense that some of the character has gone. The houses have stepped back a little way from the pavement, which is sensible since cars have replaced bikes. But the street lights are more functional and the children can't play safely any more.

CROFT STREET

WE HAVE LEFT Waun Wen and moved the short distance to the top of High Street. Here we find one of the lost scenes of Swansea, for the original shape of Croft Street has been squashed by the tower blocks of Dyfatty. The end of Croft Street where it joins High Street still survives, but the rest has gone and it has taken its stories with it. The earlier photograph was taken in 1959 and the place where the photograph was taken has disappeared behind the undergrowth that surrounds the flats.

Ordinary people lived on Croft Street. Here you would find a butcher, a charwoman, a fish hawker and an errand boy. Croft Street seems to have accommodated those who serviced the needs of a growing and needy population. They came from all over the country, drawn by the prospect of work.

Conditions in the nineteenth century, however, were particularly poor. This far up High Street it was impossible to access clean water. The residents used wells and cesspits. Mortality rates were higher here than elsewhere in the town. The local priest, Father Matthew, was compelled to write a letter entitled 'A Wail from Little Ireland' to the *Cambrian Newspaper*

in March 1866. He describes the inadequacy of public hygiene in the area. 'The condition of Croft Street is an instance where the evil existed in an aggravated degree.' Inhabitants died off amidst the accumulated filth of past generations. Matthew also claimed that money allocated to improve the area had instead been spent in the west – a rather familiar complaint in Swansea over the years.

It was a place with an unfortunate history. In 1875 poor Thomas Evans, aged two, was burnt to death when his pinafore caught fire when his mother popped out to visit the neighbours. In 1903 the Wroe family were overcome by fumes from a leak in the gas main outside their house. Even though they knew something was wrong, they continued in their attempts to light the fire until they couldn't face it any more and managed to stagger out into the street. Neighbours helped revive them.

We will now turn away from the city centre and head along the west side of the River Tawe.

CWM ROAD

A SHORT WAY along Llangyfelach Street you can turn right on to Cwm Road. This was once an important road. with a tramway that brought coal from pits in Cwmbwrla. It used horse-drawn trucks that ran along tracks down to the wharves by the side of the river on the Strand. By the time the photograph was taken in 1966 they had gone and the terraced houses you can see were going to be demolished. They had served their time and they were in decay. No chimney pots, just holes in the roof and no future.

There have been interesting changes here. There are crumbling steps leading up to the terraced houses in the older picture. Today there are steps leading down from the street.

Hafod Primary School on Odo Street is still there behind, looking down on them. On the other side of the road you can see the original nineteenth-century retaining wall. But the houses that were there have gone, and new buildings now stretch down the road to the very low bridge that goes under Neath Road.

Today it is a residential area. The satellite dishes indicate that the houses have become flats and they provide a home to many. Clearly it is a much more efficient use of space. The area is much calmer now, more hospitable. In the past it was always a volatile area. Back in 1879 two residents, Robert and Ann Wych, robbed a seaman, William Griffiths, and threw him into the river. The street led down on to the Strand and, as we shall see, that was a place where life was lived on the edge.

The original back gardens were overgrown and overshadowed. Today the houses have their own concrete areas. The street has gained cleanliness and hygiene; disease and squalor have gone. Whatever romantic vision we may have of the past, we should never underestimate the improvements that have been made to the quality of the lives of the people who live in such areas.

And in case it is of interest to you, I should mention that the earlier photograph was taken on 6/6/66.

EATON ROAD

WE HAVE NOW moved north, into Brynhyfryd. Robert Eaton was a banker in the days when bankers were respected, and such was his prominence that a road in the industrial heart of Swansea was named after him. His has always been a grand road, wider than absolutely necessary, running parallel to Llangyfelach Road. Once there were plans to build a canal down the middle of it. Instead there were tramlines.

   The picture dates from 1934 and looks dark and forbidding. The surface of the road seems to glisten with rain and those poisons that fell from the sky in the smoke. It was a world that no one ever thought would change; in a landscape no one ever imagined could be restored.

If you went to the top of the road and turned right you would very soon find yourself in the industrial wasteland of the Lower Swansea Valley. You could then go along Cwm Level Road, known locally as the Black Road because of the coal dust that washed down to it from the pits. You would get a sense of the smell, the smoke, the furnaces and the danger of working life in Hafod and Landore, underneath the looming mass of Pentremawr tip.

It came to pass in days of yore
The Devil chanced upon Landore
Quoth he, 'By all this fume and stink
I can't be far from home, I think.'

It is not the greatest poem you will ever read, but you can see what the writer was getting at.

Look at the modern photograph. The houses and the shape of the street are still recognisable. But it is much more comfortable, more developed, and more tended. Look at the chimneys in the houses at the end of the road; we are certainly in the right place. Windows have moved and one wall on the right appears higher; the other could be the same. The shops have different uses now. The one with the white awning today is the local clairvoyant's. Could they, with their intuition and necromancy, have ever predicted how much the world on Eaton Road would have changed in eighty years?

NEATH ROAD

WE HAVE GONE along Cwm Level Road and turned left on to Neath Road. We are in Plasmarl and it is 1937.

Written on the back of the photograph are the words 'Tram Abandonment'. What a quaint expression for what is regarded as an act of vandalism by some today. Yet it must have seemed such a good idea in 1937 when the photo was taken – to rip up those old-fashioned rails and give freedom of movement and expression to the car. There is a hint at what is to come in the garage on the right. Jeffrey's Commercial Motors, alone but pointing to the future. There are far more garages which stretch along Neath Road today. Of course, in retrospect the removal of tramlines was a big mistake. But at the time they seemed to represent the past. We yearn for such choices now.

The escape from the tracks was a seductive illusion. The road now is busy and so it has been calmed. Now we have the bendy bus along this road, pretending to be a tram but perhaps without the character. It is highly unpopular to some but very efficient to those of us who use it. You can see one approaching in the distance – our purple solution to urban transport needs, but one which doesn't seem to inspire the affection that the trams always did.

Those big concrete slabs seem to be an attempt to bury the past. Coal merchants, seen on the left, do not call quite so often, but you can't ever hide the past completely. The bus stop hasn't moved an inch.

At one point this was the industrial heartland of Swansea – a road, a canal bringing coal down from Llansamlet to the wharves along the river, and the factories. In 1873 you could find one of the world's four largest steelworks just along this road. In the distance you can see the faint outline of the chimneys in Morriston. They brought wealth for some and dirt for everyone. Today everything is so much greener – and healthier.

TAN Y LAN TERRACE

WE HAVE LEFT Neath Road, gone up Clyndu Street, and stopped at the top to look back at where we have come.

One of the notable experiences in Swansea, which only locals know about, is the trip up Trewyddfa Road, between Morriston and Cwm Level Road in Landore. It provides the most magnificent views of Swansea. You can look down all the way to the sea and up along the river valley into the hills. On a clear day it is a wonderful sight, with everything laid out beneath you.

From the road you can capture the very essence of Swansea – that unique combination of urban living with industry and commerce and people, which sits alongside cultivated land and the wildness of the hills. In the distance too you can see Devon, another world, far away.

You are standing on Tan y Lan Terrace and the first picture is from 1929. You can look down to Morriston and see the smog gathering from the shadowy factories. The houses seem dark and unwelcoming. There was a particular contrast, however, just round the corner on the left, on Lan Street. This was where you would find Phillip Matthews' Grocery Store. It was known as Castle Stores because of its fine and rather incongruous crenellations.

To the right you can see the beginnings of Trewyddfa Road, heading uphill. This is the Graig, one side of a typical glacial valley, and the road was once an unmade track glued to the hillside. Sandstone has been quarried from here over the years to build most of the local buildings. The unparalleled view down on to the copperworks is remembered in the name of the Smelter's Arms, halfway along the road.

Today the entrance to Trewyddfa Road has been moved, in order to provide a gentler incline up the steep hill.. It is now behind where both photographers stood. I can recommend it as a worthwhile detour. On a clear day there is nowhere better to go.

VICARAGE ROAD

OUR TOUR HAS now taken us a short distance west to the Vicarage Road/ Pentrepoeth Road/Clasemont Road crossroads, and I was lucky to find it so quiet – a rare occurrence these days. The first thing you notice is that the junction hasn't changed a great deal. The pavement in 1929 (when this picture was taken) was wider than it is today and the wall to the left has been rebuilt and remodelled. The view was more open too. Now the trees are more mature and obscure the views. What you notice are the changes we have made to accommodate the car. Today we have to manage the environment, and we have to control and slow people down.

The construction of a small roundabout was designed to ease the speed of the traffic coming down Clasemont Road, and it came in the aftermath of a horrible fatal accident. Traffic crossing the junction along Vicarage Road has more of a chance these days.

We are slaves to the car, to the need to move and to connect. We live further away from where we work than our predecessors did and we have become obsessed with journey time. Yet we appear to move more slowly than ever. When the motorway which runs parallel to Pentrepoeth Road is closed, the traffic is diverted and the whole road seizes up completely. How those of us who live in Morriston love those days.

The road is constantly busy, a main suburban route and a reminder that Swansea was never built with the car in mind. Pentrepoeth Road takes you down to Morriston Cross and on towards Llansamlet. Clasemont Road takes you to the DVLA and the west. Head that way and you will eventually arrive in Llangyfelach, for centuries the site of one of the most important fairs in south Wales, held on St David's Day.

Beneath the surface Morriston is littered with mine workings – plans show an underground canal near the top of Cwmbath Road, which is back where we came from on Vicarage Road.

You are never far from the past in Swansea, and as we head down to the river valley and cross to the other side, we are connecting with one of the oldest routes in the city.

YNYSTANGLWST BRIDGE

YOU NEED TO head for the giant Ynysforgan roundabout, then on
the old road to Clydach and then take a right turn at the roundabout
to Ynysforgan Park. It is here that the engineers took this fascinating
picture of the important bridge that crosses the River Tawe, lying
between Morriston and Clydach. Lots of people use the bridge as a
shortcut to avoid the busy motorway roundabout or to drive to Lon Las
and Birchgrove. What you see in the earlier picture, taken in 1931, is an
older bridge, aging dangerously by the looks of it. It was replaced by a
new bridge which was opened a year later.

This bridge is one of the oldest fatures of Swansea shpwn in the book.
There is a long history to this part of the city. The name of the bridge
remembers Tanglwst, the name of both the wife and the daughter of
the most important resident of the area. This was Hopcyn ap Tomos
who was born in 1330. He collected Welsh literature which was copied

to become *The Red Book of Hergest*, a very important collection of poems, stories and herbal remedies. He was reputed to be an expert in bardic prophecy, though the changes that Swansea has experienced would have, I am sure, challenged his particular talents.

This has always been an important bridging point. In medieval times it was the route up to the monastery at Llangyfelach, where there was a guesthouse. A type of service station I suppose.

These days, people walk and cycle along the riverbank down to the estuary, a path that has been constructed through Swansea's industrial heritage.

This stopped being a pedestrian bridge some time ago. Now it is a single-lane road bridge; as you wait for your turn to cross you can admire the view. The river now is clean and clear and fishermen gather here in the dusk of a summer's eve before descending to the bank in pursuit of the local sewin.

LLANSAMLET

WE ARE ON the east side of the river now and have travelled a little way downstream, to a place which has changed beyond all recognition.

The date of the older photograph is Tuesday, 12 November 1929, and it records the time when Llansamlet flooded. It isn't easy to place today but the best way to orientate oneself is to use the hills which are obscured by the trees. Both photographs were taken from the site of the gasworks, on the edge of the roundabout at Fendrod Way.

In 1929 there was torrential rain. It started on a Sunday and dampened the Armistice Ceremony in town, then continued throughout the night and the following day. By the end of it, Cray Reservoir had risen 5ft in a single day. It was the highest recorded rainfall for twenty-nine years. The *South Wales Daily Post* said the rain was 'relentless in its very ceaselessness', which is not the sort of journalism you can get away with today.

It has always been a marshy area and flooding had happened before – but not on this scale. Sandbags didn't work. A family placed their furniture on the kitchen table but by morning the dresser was floating near the ceiling. One man lost sixteen pigs. There were cats in trees, chickens on roofs and drowned geese. A sick man sleeping downstairs was found floating in his bed in 3ft of water. At the Travellers Rest, at the back of which is the original photograph, the piano was left in the water which meant, obviously, that a continuation of business was impossible. Food was taken to the stranded guests via plank bridges to their bedrooms.

Work was stopped at the Worcester Works (which you can see in the distance) since there was 2ft of water in the offices.

The road level had been raised, as you might just be able to see, but the houses had not been. The residents believed that it had formed a dam to retain the water. The engineers denied that this was the case, but the continuous rape of the river valley over a century certainly destroyed the natural drainage system.

The Mayor was brought to see 'the pitiable domestic conditions and responded with sympathetic insight.' Residents, however, could only answer his questions 'in toneless monosyllables.'

The scene was described as 'a huge lake, rippling serenely in the morning sun'. Today, in the early evening, the same scene is a sea of barely moving traffic.

MANSEL ROAD

FOR THIS REMARKABLE photograph our journey takes us up the hill
above the river valley; it is a real insight into what Swansea once looked
like. This is Mansel Road in Bonymaen, grey and forbidding, looking
down to the industry which lies hidden in the smog. The year is 1926.
The building you see, looking stranded and forlorn, is St Margaret's
Church. It sits on a bleak, unappealing hillside above the smoke of the
industry that poisoned the whole area. In the photograph it looks toxic –
which is exactly what it was.

Look at the road surface; as yet unmade. What does this tell us about
traffic, or about people's expectations? Once the road was made, houses
were built to surround the church.

The great advantage for the residents was that they had an unrivalled
view of the industrial wasteland around them. It was a superb vantage
point to take in the glories of the Hafod Tip on the opposite side of the
river, with its 10 million tons of slag and ashes – but only of course
when the smoke parted.

But for the people this was their world. There was nothing unusual in it.
A landscape polluted for almost 200 years was their home. Copper, zinc,
tin, sulphuric acid and arsenic floated in the air around them.

The whole valley below Mansel Road was ravaged by satanic sulphur and subject to erosion which stripped away the topsoil and leached poisons into the ground. In the gardens of Mansel Road nothing would ever grow. It is no surprise that there was deep resentment against those who destroyed a beautiful valley and substituted it with a dangerous barren desert.

Today the area has been regenerated. Look at the picture and orientate yourself by St Margaret's – it is just beyond the white house. There is green; the views are still extensive but much improved. Now the road features traffic calming and smart, comfortable houses. Now there is grass to mow and trees to climb. But many generations of children in Swansea had no such things.

WHITE ROCK TIP

WE HAVE PASSED through Bonymaen and joined Pentrechwyth Road to arrive at what is today the Kilvey woodlands.

This breathtaking picture is an example of the dead landscape that the Lower Swansea Valley became. This is where our ancestors lived, amongst the largest area of industrial dereliction in Europe. It is impossible to think that people could ever live here. This was the Swansea Valley; watered by constant rain, and as fertile as the moon. The vegetation of the valley was destroyed and the high rainfall washed away any topsoil that there might have been. The area was sterile. This is the edge of the White Rock Tip in Pentrechwyth in 1968.

Wales was the world's first industrial nation; first to employ more people in industry than in agriculture. Oh yes, Wales had a huge significance in shaping the world. But we should never forget the impact of industry on the environment and upon the people.

The White Rock tip represented 200 years of dumping, an enormous pile of poison that was visible from anywhere in the valley. Its weight compacted the soil and the weather shaped it in strange ways. It became fused into alien, threatening shapes, like an eruption. Industry created huge amounts of waste which was dumped as near as possible to the works to reduce transportation costs. They developed bricks made of crushed slag, but there was so much that they could never hope to use it all. So it was left.

The tip was 33 hectares in size. It comprised 183,000 tons of copper waste and cost £129,210 to remove it in 1967–68. The waste was used to raise the level of the land to form the Enterprise Park in Llansamlet.

Much of the industrial heritage has gone now, the good as well as the bad. It is a much healthier and safer environment. Kilvey Hill Community Woodlands has been created. The Lower Swansea Valley is a more pleasant place to live but an important part of our heritage has gone too. It is hard to know whether we should mourn it.

You can see a real contrast when you study the present-day photograph. The landscape has changed completely. You look down to the Liberty Stadium in a restored valley and verdant green is now the dominant colour.

That restoration was quite a remarkable achievement and one we should never forget. It made our world a much better place.

NEW CUT BRIDGE

WE HAVE COME down Foxhole Road to St Thomas and are about to cross the river again. The photograph shows the New Cut Bridge in 1965, just before it was opened by the Secretary of State for Wales, James Griffiths.

This was the fourth bridge to be built at this point and the first one which came to form an integral part of a large roundabout – one that now distributes traffic at speed to the confusion of the timid and the wary. Of course, there are many occasions during the day when the traffic doesn't move at all. The free-flowing quality to be observed in both photographs is something of which many drivers can only dream.

The bridge hasn't changed since 1965, but what has changed are the incidentals, the bits that form the background. The bridge will be the same until it is replaced, but behind it in the earlier picture you can see the famous Weaver's building, which dominated the skyline for over eighty years. It was the first reinforced concrete building in Britain, and the first to be used as a target by the Luftwaffe. This is what the bombers trained their sights on when they came to call in the Blitz. It was so monumental that it could be seen from high in the sky. It was as attractive as an abattoir: a huge grain mill, grey and forbidding. The building was demolished in 1984 and the site is now a supermarket. On the riverbank just downstream of the bridge there is column of reinforced concrete from Weaver's, preserved for posterity.

You can also see the railway bridge beyond it. The pillars stand there still, a fine roosting point for seagulls, acting as a reminder of the importance of the railways in Swansea's history.

Today the skyline is much cleaner, though the bridge supports are more stained. The area is more open and welcoming. Now the view is dominated by the Millennium Tower, currently the tallest building in Wales, and the dome of Salubrious Place sits happily in its shadow.

THE STRAND

WE HAVE HEADED into town and then turned right to enter the Strand. It is March 1930 and there is something sinister here, amongst the neglected decay. It seems to be a threatening world, one in which people don't seem to care about very much at all. On the left was the entrance to the North Dock. This was where Swansea met the outside world and sometimes that was a dangerous place to be. Desperate sailors from all over the world came spilling off the boats and there were others on shore eager to part them from their money. This was one of Swansea's faces and it wasn't always the most attractive.

Businesses moved there for the opportunities it presented. Mrs Cohen's pawnbroking business was here and Captain Paul Smith had a factory which produced ship's biscuit. You can see a meat importer's store and an engineering workshop, the Inkerman Works. The strand was where you came to buy sails or the ships on which to hang them. And it was a place of petty crime and human disasters. In 1861 there was a request to install lighting on the Strand to 'deter immoral congregations'. You will understand why. In 1879 Elizabeth Thomas, aged sixteen, worked here; she was 'an orange seller by day and loose girl by night'. It is where Hanna Sparkes and John Goss were arrested for 'indecent conduct in 1868.' In 1866 William Eastman was prosecuted for having 'a foul

and offensive privy'. George Hobbs was injured after a fall into the Strand sewer in 1849, and David Davies, aged five, died after falling into the dry dock. Mary Norman from Devon was found drunk in the Strand in 1876. She had been in Swansea eight months and had already been imprisoned nine times. In the same year, a young boy, Edward Hopkins was burnt to death in a shed. Andrew Duncan beat his wife Emma to death with a flat iron in 1872 and was sent to Broadmoor. This was truly life on the edge.

In front you can see the junction with Green Dragon Lane, its name alone marking Swansea out as a place apart. Today the Strand is forgotten and neglected, no longer at the front of anyone's mind. But it is still a place where you would not willingly choose to linger.

WELCOME LANE

A LITTLE FURTHER up the Strand you will find Welcome Lane. You might think it an incongruous name for somewhere with an undistinguished past based upon disorder and drunkenness, where sailors were arrested for fighting – an unsettling place. It has always been proud to be at the cutting edge of Swansea's history and has always provided a welcome, of sorts, to its visitors.

Welcome Lane was constantly modified. Houses were cleared in the lane in the nineteenth century as a precaution against cholera outbreaks. Like much of Swansea it was tight and narrow, a jumble of buildings leaning against each other. It was widened in the twentieth century to ease access down to the Strand. So it was always a place with an interesting mix of commercial and industrial properties, in addition to the public houses, and the occasional private home.

Welcome Lane linked them all with the town city. And the air-raid shelter you see here was designed for them all.

In 1965 the engineers turned up to photograph the air-raid shelter before they knocked it down.

Obviously it was designed for safety and protection during the Second World War, but there were problems. People would turn up with deck chairs, which rather exercised the ARP officer. In September 1940 he found that people turned up intending to make themselves comfortable. They brought pillows and blankets too. Not only that, but one air-raid shelter seemed to have been transformed into a fish 'n' chip bar. These people were obviously not taking the war seriously enough. Sadly, they would soon have to. German bombers destroyed the town in the three-day Blitz in February 1941.

Now the air-raid shelter has disappeared completely. There is only a patch of grass opposite where the North Dock used to be. It was once so very important but is now forgotten. Now Welcome Lane is a busy road that allows the traffic to come up from the river. The newly introduced and elaborate traffic system enables one to brave the intricacies of the Kingsway. People wait for the lights to change at the top of the hill, looking about them absent-mindedly, without realising the history of this short and undistinguished road.

ST MARY'S

YOU HAVE GONE up Welcome Lane, turned left and then turned right by the castle and wandered through Castle Gardens. Now you have arrived at St Mary's Church in the heart of Swansea. It was the most important church in Swansea and provides a reminder of the original shape of the settlement. The castle is at one end of the settlement on a defensive mound and the church is at the other. Of course St Mary's has a long history. It was erected on its present site in about 1328 as the 'Church of the blessed Marye of Sweyns' and today people from the other side of the world turn up, strum guitars and sing evangelical songs, loudly. What an inclusive community we have become.

The oldest surviving artefact in St Mary's lies sheltered beneath a carpet to the left of the altar. It is the black marble stone that once covered the grave of Sir Hugh Johnnys, who was Knight Marshal of England and died in 1485.

In 1739 the roof of St Mary's fell in on a Sunday morning before the waiting congregation had entered. It was rebuilt and then renovated in 1882 when the slums alongside the church in Frog Street and Cross Street were cleared. It was then taken down and rebuilt in 1896. Then the bombers came.

The older photograph was taken in 1938. Look closely and you can see a man on the first roof as the row of houses is taken apart. At the far end you can make out an advert for Oxo, proud sponsors of the 1908 Olympics and still an essential ingredient of the pre-war lifestyle.

You are looking at a row of houses on Calvert Street which have since disappeared. This is where taxis queue today to take home exhausted shoppers. Our very own Quadrant Shopping Precinct is at the end of the street.

And it is in the corner of the window above the entrance to the Quadrant, hidden away where no one can see him, that you will find the Swansea Devil. He is an objectionable landmark to some; a wooden sculpture said to resemble the Devil, but looking more like a woodland pixie. It was allegedly commissioned by the architect who failed to win the contract to redesign the church in 1896. The sculpture was placed to stare at the church and it was said that it would live to see the church destroyed – and of course it did in the Blitz in 1941. St Mary's was a smoking shell and the Devil was untouched. Look just above the canopy to the left as you go in and you will see him, grinning like a pixie.

OXFORD STREET

WE HAVE WANDERED back through Castle Square, past the overly large and smelly fast food restaurant, to the end of Oxford Street. I stood there amongst suspicious shoppers, waiting to take a picture without intruding on their privacy.

Oxford Street has been through so much. It is a place we all take for granted and yet one which has been in a constant state of change. Look, for example, at the traffic lights in the early photograph which mark the junction with Waterloo Street, which is now largely lost.

Oxford Street was reborn after the war, but then it had to be. What you see in the old photograph was completely destroyed. Photographs in the aftermath of the Blitz merely show shapeless piles of broken

bricks, unrecognisable. In this picture from the Swansea Archive you can see the focal point of a life that ceased in February 1941. The picture is undated but was taken at some point in the 1920s. It was 8.30 a.m., and in typical fashion a man had turned up on the left (just behind the Belisha beacon) to start digging up the pavement.

The modern picture was taken over ninety years later. Of course, the shape of the town has changed and it isn't possible to get into the same position as before. The trees are a pleasing addition but they do rather get in the way in situations like this.

Our expectations are different too. We expect a livelier, more entertaining space outside the shops, so there are always stalls and displays. On this occasion there was a promotional vehicle from Gower College, a demonstration of beach tennis as part of some kind of summer festival, and a man offering to buy unwanted jewellery. In the earlier photograph everything is less cluttered. Then it was a street with cars, trams and pedestrians.

Today our expectation is that Swansea will host national chain stores. It is important that our city centre looks like everyone else's; otherwise we will be regarded as the poor relations, missing out on what other people take for granted. Of course in earlier times this was much less important. Oxford Street in those days featured such fine shops as Lassam S. Evans and his mantle warehouse, the umbrella maker Charles Dickens, and of course Madame Dalma, phrenologist.

When you think about it, I am sure there is still a public there for them, with the right marketing.

DILLWYN STREET

A PLEASANT WANDER along the shops in Oxford Street brings you to this point; the junction between Oxford Street and Dillwyn Street. It would be nice to think that the eye is drawn by two things – the beautiful, stylish traffic lights and Cash Hardware Stores with its fine collection of buckets outside. However, it is the advertisement for salad cream that dominates the view and which worried the council. It was March 1950 and salad cream was much too exciting. That is why they took the photograph. It was far too intrusive.

This is Dillwyn Street, which was built in 1850 and was then on the very edge of the town. In a way its status has never really changed. That is where it has always been, on the edge of things. That is perhaps why ventures like restaurants have never really succeeded down there. As you can see, the transformation from a Pets' Supplies Stores to a restaurant was not a sustained success.

In 1950 the road seemed more relaxed and peaceful. You see the ubiquitous bicycle against the kerb and no apparent fear that it will be knocked over. There are men in hats, boys in shorts, and small unthreatening cars.

Today it is more of a traffic thoroughfare – part of the way in which movement through the city is more obviously directed. It links the Kingsway with Oystermouth Road, the marina and the Civic Centre, through its carefully painted lanes. It is the haunt of the bendy bus which, from this point onwards, takes students from all over the world from their lodgings in Sandfields and Mount Pleasant on to the university.

Some things haven't changed. Look at the upper storeys of the houses at the top of the street. If only that row of three shops sheltering in the arches was allowed to become a monolithic structure which would dwarf everything. At one time the estate agent's was a frozen food store – business concerns united by the way in which they can fill your soul with a penetrating chill.

Incidentally, in the interests of clarity I feel I must point out that the dark building is a nightclub and offers in its name no judgement about the current state of our city. If, however, I am wrong and it does, then there are significant elements of contemporary life in Swansea that pass me by.

ST HELEN'S ROAD

WE HAVE GONE to the top of Dillwyn Street and have turned left to look at No.12
St Helen's Road. In 1941 it was the Gainsborough Studio, owned by Jack Thomas, who is not
only a photographer but also an artist – such talent. This simple photograph brings together
three important elements of life in Swansea in an unexpected way. It represents a journey
through the past 170 years and, as a result, this is one of my favourite spreads.

In the first place it reminds us of the central part Swansea played in the development
of photography in the nineteenth century. John Dillwyn Llewelyn, who owned the grand
house at Penllergaer, was married to Emma Talbot, a cousin of William Henry Fox Talbot,
the inventor of the negative-positive photographic process. The whole family became
enthusiastic photographers and left behind a legacy of fascinating pictures. Their friend
Calvert Richard Jones took the earliest dated photograph in Wales in 1841, of Margam
Abbey. Of course, as time went on it became less of a rich man's hobby and more of a
commercial venture, and gave a career to people like Jack Thomas.

Secondly, the picture represents the determination and the bravado of the people of
Swansea during the Blitz in 1941. Business as usual it says, whilst all around the city
centre has been reduced to rubble. Swansea came under attack on forty-three occasions.
The first attack was a raid on Danygraig on 27 June 1940. By the time of the last attack
on 16 February 1943, 384 people had died, 859 were injured and the city centre needed

to be rebuilt. Jack Thomas was as close to the destruction as it was possible to be, but his studio remained intact.

Of course, the world has moved on and No.12 St Helen's Road has become a fine Indian restaurant. As such, it represents the growing multiculturalism of the city. People from all over the world have brought us welcome colour and diversity, enriched our lives and made Swansea a twenty-first-century city.

The windows upstairs in the original picture had been blocked, perhaps to form a dark room. Today those windows have been restored to their original purpose and perhaps as a result they represent a restored openness and confidence about Swansea that we should cherish.

SWANSEA GENERAL
AND EYE HOSPITAL

NOW WE ARE at the far end of St Helen's Road, at the intersection with Brynymor Road and Beach Street. In this undated nineteenth-century photograph we are looking at the entrance to the Swansea General and Eye Hospital. At that time this was at the junction of St Helen's Road and Phillip's Parade. Today Phillips Parade is blocked to traffic by bollards.

    The hospital opened in 1869. It cost £14,000 to build on what, at the time, were open fields on the edge of town. You can see this, because the early photograph pre-dates the laying of tramlines. In the background to the left you can see the undeveloped ridge of Townhill. The building of the hospital

was approved by no less a figure than Florence Nightingale. It was a fine structure, the building of which inspired huge civic pride. It was a gesture – an investment by the people into the support systems in their own community. People came to look at it with pleasure. We can see the prosperous before it: ladies with parasols, a man with a dog, and a fine postbox.

In 1865 the papers carried lists of those who had subscribed money for its building – famous Swansea names like Eaton, Vivian and Dillwyn. Other benefactors included the Harbour Trust and the copperworks. There was a sense of a community coming together for the common good. Later on, legacies would be left in wills. There was no health service and so a hospital run on voluntary contributions was the only access to medical care that many people had. It was built for fifty beds but this was soon found to be completely inadequate, particularly because of the number of people injured in industrial accidents. After all, there were more than 600 furnaces in the Swansea Valley alone.

The hospital sustained some damage in the war when the operating theatre was bombed and then a ward was demolished by a blast; 300 patients were evacuated to neighbouring hospitals. But what the bombers could not achieve we managed for ourselves. The hospital was demolished in the 1980s. Only the clock tower and the façade remain, but the trees have thrived and provide extensive discretion for those who reside in what is now a retirement home, which you can see if you peek around the trees. But please, don't stare.

ST HELEN'S

WE HAVE TRAVELLED past the Guildhall and arrived at the St Helen's Rugby and
Cricket Ground, about half a mile up Oystermouth Road from the crazy golf course we
visited earlier in the book. St Helen's was opened in 1873 as the home of the Swansea
Rugby Club, which has been there ever since, and has hosted cricket matches and
annual firework displays. And in the late nineteenth century there was a track for
cycle racing too.

The earlier photograph is from 1925 and opens a window into another time. The
tramlines are visible to the left, in front of the advertising hoardings. You can still
see the famous East Stand with its atmospheric cloisters, through which a woman
is about to push a pram. It was demolished and replaced by a more functional and
less-loved structure.

St Helen's has a proud history – the only ground on which Australia, South Africa
and New Zealand have been beaten at both cricket and rugby, which must count for
something.

And of course in 1968 Gary Sobers, West Indies legend and at the time captain
of Nottinghamshire, hit six sixes in one over off the bowling of Swansea's very own
Malcolm Nash. Of course, Sobers was caught once but the fielder, Roger Davis,

carried the ball over the boundary so it didn't count. The fateful over was sad on two counts. First that it was televised, so there was no hiding place, and secondly for the fact that Malcolm Nash is remembered for this moment of madness when the ball kept disappearing down King Edward's Road and not for his other considerable achievements.

But Sobers was not the only important player to have appeared at the ground for either sport. Let us consider the great W.J. Bancroft. He was groundsman, just like his father before him, but he was also a Welsh International rugby full back and Glamorgan's first professional cricketer.

Oystermouth Road is twice as wide as it once was. This is to accommodate the changing face of Swansea, with more people living in the west. The whole road we can see in the 1925 photograph is now merely the in-bound carriageway. It was unusually quiet when I went to take the photograph, for it was Saturday, 17 March 2012, and Wales was securing the rugby union Grand Slam by beating the French in Cardiff. Sport does have its benefits, now and again.

MANSEL STREET

THE MANSELS ARE an old Swansea family, and Mansel Street is that bit which joins Walter Road and De la Beche Street. We have turned back towards the centre of Swansea and found a fine row of distinguished houses which in appearance haven't changed much, although the street has more of a run-down air to it now. The section we are looking at has Verandah Terrace in the middle of it and leads down to the Albert Hall.

It seems to have been a place of some urban comfort, to which aging sea captains retired in the nineteenth century. But Mansel Street was also a home to private businesses.

Mrs Jenkins' Ladies School was once at No.25. At No.44 Zitella Tomkins was giving painting lessons in July 1878. Sadly, by the end of August 1878, all the contents of No.44 were for sale.

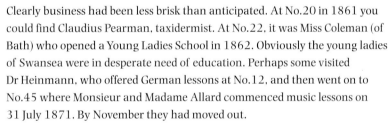

Clearly business had been less brisk than anticipated. At No.20 in 1861 you could find Claudius Pearman, taxidermist. At No.22, it was Miss Coleman (of Bath) who opened a Young Ladies School in 1862. Obviously the young ladies of Swansea were in desperate need of education. Perhaps some visited Dr Heinmann, who offered German lessons at No.12, and then went on to No.45 where Monsieur and Madame Allard commenced music lessons on 31 July 1871. By November they had moved out.

Mr C.W. Smith was proud to announce that he was the sole agent for Gossage's Patent Soap. He should have offered a discount to Philip Walters who, in 1857, was charged with having an overflowing cesspit – he said it wasn't his turn to empty it since he shared it with his neighbour. In 1859 James Pengelly was accused of ill-treating a donkey in Mansel Street. Today there are offices and flats and small business concerns. One hopes that they do not have to confront the sadness that these houses contain in their memories.

In 1886 Mansel Street had a very bad year. At No.66 three daughters of the late John Edmunds died within four months of each other – Ellen, Rose and Catherine. William Hughes, the vet, lived at No.36. His daughter Edith, eleven months old, died in March. His wife Elizabeth died on Boxing Day and their infant daughter Ethel Florence, just nine weeks old, died the following day.

ALBERT HALL

AT THE JUNCTION of Mansel Street and Cradock Street you will find the Albert Hall. It was opened in 1864 – the most famous of all Swansea music halls t. Built in 1864 by the Swansea Public Hall Co. Ltd for £4,650, it had a spacious orchestra pit with an organ and could seat 2,600 people, making it the largest public hall in town. It was also used as a place of worship on a Sunday. They did wedding receptions too. The stone portico has long gone and its time as a cinema eventually came to an end. It became the Top Rank Club, famous for its bingo. Now it is neglected and

abandoned; such a fall from grace, especially when you consider that in 1875 the music hall played host to the Blondinette Melodists – 'ten young ladies with golden locks'. My whole life has been lived in the shadow of my disappointment at missing their performance.

On the occasion of the photograph in 1929, as you can see the Albert Hall was featuring the newly released The *Trespasser*, starring Gloria Swanson. It was promoted as her first talking picture, although it was released in both silent and talkie versions, just in case dialogue and conversation didn't catch on. In fact, her performance led to an Oscar nomination as Best Actress (she was beaten by Norma Shearer in *The Divorcee*. The girl was robbed).

There always seem to be men with ladders in these pictures and yet here it looks as if Gloria herself is on her way up to join a man with a flat cap. Perhaps she should have dressed more sensibly.

Today the Albert Hall has an air of neglect. Not quite as much as that which embraces the sadly decaying hulk of the Palace Theatre up by the station, but you feel that the building deserves more. Its glories and attractiveness have been stolen. Now thriving shrubs grow from both structures, slowly pulling apart the masonry of our heritage.

89

CRADOCK STREET

WE HAVE TURNED right at the Albert Hall to take in, briefly, the glories of Cradock Street. In the present-day photoraph you can see an unexceptional modern street. But Cradock Street has a long history and in the past it was a street with very mixed use. It was here that Mrs Habakkuk had a school for the education of young ladies in the nineteenth century. And just in case you had some money to spare, Captain Jones of Cradock Street in 1849 had a couple of llamas for sale. They obviously took up a lot of space in a small house.

The spelling given to the street varies, seemingly at random; sometimes two ds, sometimes one. But its position never alters. Today Cradock Street carries with it a sense of the past. It was not as damaged as other parts of town, and it retains some hints of character in comparison with the bland uniformity of that which surrounds it. You can see on the right in both photographs the gables of houses untouched by the bombers. These are emblems of the past to which Swansea people cling desperately; a sign that the old town was once much more attractive than the modern city. The Albert Hall is still there, still a listed building, and still has shrubs growing in the gutter.

The undated, early twentieth-century photograph is very atmospheric. The tramlines take your eye and lead you back to a tram, advertising Ben Evans' Store; as most of them seemed to. Alongside you can see a horse and cart. The portico of the Albert Hall is visible, beneath which a man watches the photographer. Beneath the gables we appear to have an early jogger, with hat. A man, also in a hat and wearing a dirty apron, watches on. I am confident that neither of them would ever have anticipated that one day there would be a nail and hair studio here. Their jealousy would have been hard to contain.

One of the Swansea treasures lost when St Mary's Church was bombed in the Blitz was the tomb of Sir Matthew and Catherine Craddock. She had previously been married to Perkin Warbeck, who was hanged in 1499 for plotting to overthrow Henry VII. He should have denied it because he had a perfect alibi – he should have said he had gone off to have his nails done.

DE LA BECHE STREET

WE HAVE GONE back up to the Albert Hall and turned right and found ourselves on De la Beche Street, looking at Grove Place.

It was named after Sir Henry de la Beche (1796–1855), the geologist. He is remembered particularly for his reports on the state of housing in a number of towns, including Swansea. Now it is his road that we remember.

This has always been a significant area, sitting between the station and parts of the town. The tramlines you see would have taken you up towards the station, and if you turned right you would head uphill towards Mayhill and beyond.

In the photograph from 1925 Swansea looks like an alien place. It seems dark and cold. If you look closely you can see slush gathered in the gutter. There is a pavement, but there is an unappealing layer of mud encroaching on the tramlines.

The huge wall on the right is plastered with advertisements which provide a vivid insight into the past. There is a particular emphasis on meat extracts – on liquids made by boiling bones until they melted. There is an advert for Oxo and one for Bovril, both of which were trying to sustain the

popularity they had developed in the trenches of the First World War. There are adverts too for Bisto and for Birds' Egg Substitute.

This is now a very busy road junction as you can see in the modern photograph, with the central police station with the blue tiles to the left, and the Magistrates' Court to the right. You can also see the edge of the Metropolitan University's Faculty of Art and Design on the right, which was once Dynevor School. It is interesting too that Kilvey Hill is now visible to the right, since modern developments have opened up the view. Once we have negotiated the junction we will go along Alexandra Road, past the Glynn Vivian Art Gallery, and up to the station where our trip will end.

HIGH STREET STATION

WE HAVE ARRIVED at Swansea's main railway station. It was opened in 1850 at the top of the High Street, which was always traditionally the main route through the town. Now it is the place where we will end this brief tour through our heritage.

The station was built by the South Wales Railway – one of five different companies that ran the seven different stations in Victorian times. It has been renovated and extended several times and so nothing of the original building remains. Once there was a fish dock here and also a line which bypassed the terminal and went down to the former Swansea Victoria Station, which is where the leisure centre is today.

There is a sense in the older photograph from 1929 that passengers would have arrived in the middle of a busy town. That isn't the case today. Like many other cities, the shape of the place has changed and the station is less central. It doesn't always present the most positive impression for visitors to the town. Plans are underway to improve the area, but it does seem to be a losing battle at times. Look at that shop sign on the chemist's on the corner of Mariner Street. The sign 'Pure Drugs' indicates a branch of Boots. Now the building is an Espresso Bar. For me, that innocent drugs reference connects the past with the present. High Street has always been a challenging area. Little Ireland it was called; it was full of slum dwellings with too few toilets. It is still challenging today; it is the only area in the centre of Swansea with a permanent police presence.

Stations are also places of departure and it is at this point that our journey into our heritage will end. And as I conclude this book I find myself thinking about the man standing on the awning halfway up the ladder. Who was he? What became of him? What part did he play in the history of our town? An important part I am sure, just as all of us have in our own ways. And I also reflect that some things we regard as modern have been around for a long time. Look carefully at the advertisement to the far left of that ladder. What is it advertising? An 'Evening Express to Paris'. Proof if ever it were needed that we should never underestimate the past.

And now, together, all of us who have read this book will head into Swansea's future. We don't know what it will bring, but it will be fun finding out.

Other titles published by The History Press

Swansea in 100 Dates
GEOFF BROOKES

Experience 100 key dates that shaped Swansea's history, highlighted its people's genius (or silliness) and embraced the unexpected. Featuring an amazing mix of social, criminal and sporting events, this book reveals a past that will fascinate, delight and even shock both residents and visitors of the city.

978 0 7524 9909 3

Fishing Around the Bristol Channel
MIKE SMYLIE & SIMON COOPER

The Bristol Channel is a compelling area of the nation's seas to discover. In this book, renowned maritime historian Mike Smylie, along with Simon Cooper, experts in the field, delve into the variety of fishing methods used in the past and present around this coastline. Accompanied by previously unseen photographs and drawings, the authors present a fascinating account of the lives of the 'Severn Sea' fishermen. This book is a must for fishing enthusiasts and those with an interest in local history.

978 0 7524 5792 5

Bloody Welsh History: Swansea
GEOFF BROOKES

This book explores the hidden stories of Swansea's long and dangerous past – stories of death, shipwreck and murder. From Viking raids to English attacks, deadly diseases, factory riots, slums, cholera and Nazi bombs, you'll never see the city in the same way again. What happened to 150 elephant tusks? Why were all those men trapped in the hold when the *Caesar* hit the rocks at Pwlldu? Come to that, what happened to those suits of armour? Compiled by Swansea's own Geoff Brookes, read it if you dare!

978 0 7524 8053 4

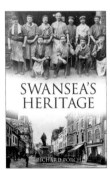

Swansea's Heritage
RICHARD PORCH

In *Swansea's Heritage* Richard Porch brings together a series of events, buildings and personalities which have created and maintained Swansea's character from the Middle Ages to the present day. From the Vikings and Victorian sea captains to Harry and Benjamin Davies, the Upper Bank Coppermen, this compendium also features a geological heritage trail round the city, in addition to an exhaustive timeline of events that have contributed to Swansea's development over the centuries.

978 0 7524 4559 5

Visit our website and discover thousands of other History Press books.

www.thehistorypress.co.uk